Magnificent Mind Listens Mindfully

Ellen Arnold

Illustrations by Deborah Farber

Zephyr Press®
REACHING THEIR HIGHEST POTENTIAL
Tucson, Arizona

Acknowledgments

—To Jonah, whose ability to listen to stories is awesome—

Creating books takes work, but when you have a great team, the process can be joyful. Deborah Farber's picture smart part helped develop my ideas into a wonderful visual presence. Marti Arnold's word- and number-smart parts were an invaluable asset in helping me be clear, concise, and consistent. Without their patience, ideas, and support, this project would still be in my mind rather than in your hands.

Magnificent Mind Listens Mindfully

Grades K–4

Printed in the United States of America

ISBN 1-56976-112-4

Editor: Bonnie Lewis
Design & Production: Daniel Miedaner
Cover Design: Daniel Miedaner
Illustrations: Deborah Farber

Published by
Zephyr Press
P.O. Box 66006
Tucson, Arizona 87528-6006
http://zephyrpress.com
http://giftsforteachers.com

Library of Congress Cataloging-in-Publication Data

Arnold, Ellen, 1944-
Magnificent Mind listens mindfully / by Ellen Arnold ; illustrated by Deborah Farber.
p. cm.
ISBN 1-56976-112-4 (alk. paper)
1 Listening—Study and teaching. 2. Multiple intelligences. 3. Learning strategies. I. Farber, Deborah, ill. II. Title.

LB1065 .A79 2000
370.15'23—dc21 00-032089

Magnificent Mind Listens Mindfully

A Note to Teachers and Parents:

Teachers expect students to listen attentively in class. But Magnificent Mind, like many students, does not know how to do this. In this book, Maggie sets off to fill her bag with strategies that will help her listen mindfully in class. ***MI Strategies for Kids,*** a teacher/parent manual, describes a lesson plan that will help make this book a most useful tool for your students.

Teacher: *Magnificent.*
Are you listening?

MM: Huh? Yes, uh, I think so.

Teacher: *Well, I just asked you a question.*

MM: I'm sorry. I guess my mind wandered.

Teacher: *Magnificent, this has become a real problem. I know you want to do well in school, but you have got to learn to take control of your mind. Now, please listen.*

MM: OK. I'll really try.

Teacher: *Now, class, today's lesson is going to be on the history of blah, blah, blah, blah . . .*

MM: How come she only talks about things that are boring? How am I supposed to really listen to all these words? My mind wants to think about things that are fun, like what a butterfly feels like, or how I am going to surprise my brother, Brilliant, with his birthday present.

Teacher: *What is the answer, Magnificent?*

MM: Huh? I am sorry, can you repeat that?

Teacher: *That's it. I have had it with you. I am going to call home and set up a time to meet with your parents. You are impossible!*

Have you ever had trouble listening like Magnificent does?

Maggie felt terrible about not listening but didn't anyone understand? She really was trying to listen. She wanted to. She tried, but then all of a sudden, without even meaning to, she found her mind was somewhere far away from where the teacher wanted it to be. By the time Magnificent realized it, she was in trouble.

As soon as Magnificent got home, she looked in her strategy bank. She found strategies for reading, strategies for math, strategies for skiing, and strategies for spelling. But she could not find any strategies for listening.

She thought about where her other strategies came from, and decided to ask her friends, the Smart Parts, if they knew any strategies that could help her with listening. She put on her strategy bank backpack and walked down Intelligence Avenue, where the Smart Parts lived. There were paths, bridges, and shortcuts that connected the different parts of this strategy-rich neighborhood.

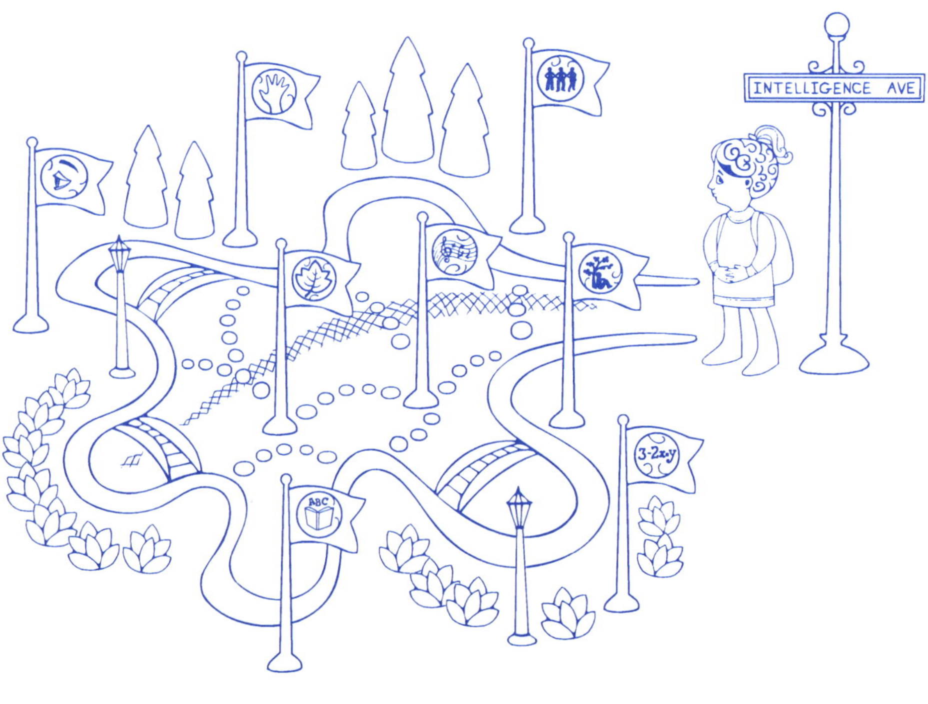

MM: Music Smart, have a heart,
Help me listen so I'll be smart.

MS: Magnificent Mind, be so kind,
Tell me what you have in mind.

MM: Can you give me some direction,
On how to better pay attention?

MS: I've had this problem. Yes, indeed.
But I know a way you can succeed.
The special thing we have to do
Is to discover rhyme for you.
If you seek to really listen,
You can find what you've been missing.

MM: But when I try to listen, my mind goes for a walk.
It doesn't want to focus on all that wordy talk.

MS: Have a focus, make a choice.
Catch the music in the voice.
Up and down, soft and loud,
Hear the music in the crowd.
Give your mind some
musical cues.
Listen for words that
YOU can use.

MM: I never thought music
could be in speech.
Maybe listening is within
my reach.

MS: You can do it, in no time.
Listen for rhythm, listen for rhyme.
Hear the changes of the tone
And what you hear can be your own.

**MM: Thank you for helping, Music Smart.
I will take your advice to heart.**

Magnificent put her new "Listen to the Rhythm" strategy in her strategy bank. She hummed as she marched further on Intelligence Avenue until she saw Picture Smart working on a painting.

MM: Wow, Picture Smart. That is a beautiful painting. You are so good with colors.

PS: Thanks, Magnificent. Are you looking for something?

MM: Yes, I am looking for listening strategies. I know I am supposed to listen in school, but I remember things better when I see them. My teacher wants me just to listen to words and not look at the pictures.

PS: I can see how that would be a problem for you. It used to be for me, but I saw a way out of it. I use pictures and symbols in my head all the time, even when I am listening. I let the words become paintbrushes. Each word adds to a picture in my head, so as someone talks, I see what they are saying.

MM: You mean you can actually see objects from words?

PS: Sure. Picture this: ***It was a dark and stormy night when the Queen's ship was due to set sail for the new land.*** Is there a picture forming in your brain?

MM: Yes. It is like a movie screen. I can see the sky with no moon, no stars, and a richly decorated golden ship rocking in the dark water.

PS: See what I mean.

MM: So can I make pictures like that when I am listening to anything?

PS: Sure. Your camera, paintbrush, colored markers, and drawing board are all waiting for you whenever you want to use them. And if you listen to the words and make pictures of them, you will remember them better.

MM: I like to draw. If I can draw in my head while I listen, maybe I'll like to listen more. Thanks, Picture Smart. I can see how this strategy will be very helpful.

Can you make up pictures in your mind when you listen? If this is hard for you, practice listening to music while you are drawing. See if the music helps you create pictures.

She put her "Draw Pictures from Words" strategy in her strategy bank.

Magnificent ran into Body Smart, who was roller blading along Intelligence Avenue.

MM: Hi Body Smart, I'm glad I caught up with you. I sure could use some coaching.

BS: I'm in training myself, so can we move while we talk? What's up?

MM: I am having trouble with listening in school. I try to sit still and listen like the teacher says, but I just can't do it. Did you ever have that trouble?

BS: Sure, all the time. You know that I don't sit still very well, ever. And listening is the worst! I need to be moving in order to listen, because moving wakes up my mind. If I sit still, my brain turns to mush.

MM: Yes, but doesn't that get you into trouble? I get told not to "bother" anyone else. I don't try to, but when I shift around, other people get upset.

BS: Oh, I know how you can build your listening muscles. Try to move without others knowing.

MM: What?

BS: Try to move your foot. Wiggle it real hard, but don't move your shoe. Tap hard, curl your toes, but as long as your shoe doesn't move, no one knows you are doing it.

MM: I can do that. It is kind of hard.

BS: Sure, but it works your muscles, keeps your mind alert, and doesn't bother anyone. Sometimes I practice running, squeezing one leg muscle and then the other, but never moving my legs so anyone can see. Try that one.

MM: That really feels like a workout. It takes concentration to do that without moving.

BS: Yes, but it really works once you get used to doing it. Anyway, that is my game plan for listening.

MM: I can see how this could be fun once I got used to it. Thanks, Body Smart. I'll let you run.

Magnificent put her "Moving without Disturbing" strategy in her strategy bank. She continued her walk, thinking about what she had learned so far. Self Smart was sitting under a tree, deep in thought.

MM: Self Smart, can I ask you a question?

SS: Sure, Magnificent. What's on your mind?

MM: I am thinking of new ways to listen better. I feel bad about what is happening in school. I really, really want to do well. But when I try to listen, my

mind just wanders away sometimes, and it is like I can't control it. Then when my teacher yells at me, I feel terrible. She thinks I don't like her, but I do. I want to listen. Do you have any advice for me?

SS: Can you think of times when you really **CAN** listen?

MM: I can listen really well to stories when they aren't boring, like stories that make me feel happy or sad.

SS: So when you tap your feelings, you aren't bored?

MM: Right.

SS: That happens to me, too. I know when I have to listen, I have to find ways to connect myself to the words I hear. I have to make them real for me. I kind of talk to myself.

MM: What do you say?

SS: Well, I make the topic more personal. I think of things like, "Why does it do that?" "Would I do the same thing?" "How will this help me in the future?" "What does this remind me of?" "How does this relate to what we learned yesterday?"

MM: But if you are asking yourself all those questions, how can you pay attention to what you are hearing?

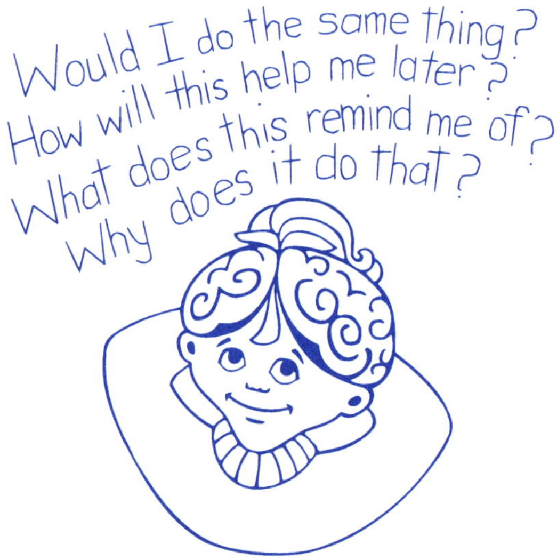

SS: I use my questions as a bridge to what I am hearing. I keep thinking about the meaning, in as many ways as I can. And if I haven't found a connection, I jot it down to reflect on later.

MM: And this helps you listen better?

SS: Sure. The hardest part of listening for me is that sometimes it goes so fast, and I can't think about it as much as I want before the teacher goes on. So I need to note it and then return to it when I have more time. That works really well.

Can you think of an example of how you personalized something in order to remember it better?

MM: Hmm. That makes sense. I'll put the "Personalize It" strategy in my bank and come back to it later, so I can really understand it. Thanks.

Magnificent proceeded across Intelligence Avenue, and as she was crossing a bridge, she heard someone talking.

WS: Super, super human, super friends, superheroes, super duper, super...

MM: Word Smart, what are you doing?

WS: I am coming up with as many words as I can that connect with super. It is a game I play a lot. Want to play?

MM: I can't right now. I am looking for listening strategies. I am having trouble listening in school.

WS: Listen. Hear. Learn. Focus. Care. Think. Ponder. Yes. I know that problem. I used to have trouble listening, but I learned some tricks.

MM: Like what?

WS: You know how much I like words. Well, I figured out a way to play with the words I hear. So when someone says something, I think of another way to say it, or other words I could use that would say it better. Sometimes, I even make up new words to go with what the other person says.

MM: Isn't that hard to do?

WS: No. It is fun. Like if the teacher said, "Take out your pencils and your books." I would think *t.o.p.a.b.*

MM: T.O.P.A.B.?

WS: Yes, that's my shortcut word for ***Take Out Pencil and Book.***

MM: You can do that so quickly?

WS: Well, I guess it took me a while to learn it, but once I started doing it, I found it was so much fun that I kept doing it. Now I don't even have to think about it. It just happens. And my new words help me remember, too.

MM: Great, Word Smart. It will take lots of practice for me to get fast at this strategy, but it sounds like a good one to add to my strategy bank. Thanks for the "Make a New Word" strategy.

MM: Number Smart, are you in the middle of something?

NS: I'm working with numbers. I like figuring out the patterns. Like 3, 6, 9, and 12. Or 4, 8, 12, 16. Want to try one? What would be the next pattern?

MM: Is it 5, 10, 15, 20?

NS: Yes. Good job, Magnificent! What's puzzling you?

MM: Do you have a pattern to help with listening? My teacher thinks I need to get better at listening in school.

NS: Well, I apply a formula, a specific series of steps. For listening, I have the HATS formula to remind me of the steps I need to use to listen effectively. 1, 2, 3, 4. H.A.T.S. Here are the steps.

1. **H**ear it and hold it
2. **A**ssociate it to something I know
3. **T**ranslate it into my strengths
4. **S**tore it so I can use it later

MM: HATS, huh? I get the steps, but I can't figure out how you use it.

NS: Okay. Let's imagine the teacher says, "Class, here is the book, *The Outsiders.* We are going to read it. What do you think it might be about?" I apply my HATS principle:

★ ***Hear it and hold it*** — "The Outsiders . . . *the outsiders . . . the outsiders . . ."*

★ ***Associate it*** — *What do I think of when I hear Outsiders? The Inside and the Outside groupings, the "in" group and the "out" group.*

★ ***Translate*** — *Well, my strength is numbers, so I would compute:*

O (outsider) = [ ]o

See how the ***o*** is outside the set? Then the next step is easy.

★ ***Store it***—my formula **[ ]*o*** is now in my favorite language—symbols!

MM: HATS. I get it! A formula. I can certainly add this to my strategy bank. Thanks.

Nature Smart was studying the clouds when Magnificent Mind found him on one of the stepping stone paths.

MM: Find anything interesting up there?

NS: Sure, I love looking at the different kinds of clouds. What's up?

MM: I am gathering some strategies for listening. But you probably don't need strategies for listening, since so much of what you do is watching.

NS: But I have had to learn to listen really well in order to truly understand nature. I listen to animal sounds and nature sounds all the time. I learn so much from listening.

MM: Like what?

NS: You know, I can almost tell when the clouds are going to change, by listening for the different sounds in the wind.

MM: How does that help you when you have to listen to people instead of the wind?

NS: Well, sometimes I pretend that I am a deer. Have you ever seen a deer standing in a field? Then as soon as it hears an unusual sound, it will raise its head, listen carefully, and decide whether to stay or run away. I try to be as good a listener as a deer.

MM: Yes. Deer really listen well, don't they?

NS: They filter sounds. They decide, ***Is this a helpful sound? Is this a dangerous sound?*** So I listen, pretending I am a deer. When I hear something that I think is helpful, I really focus on it. By pretending I am a deer, I can almost "feel" the sounds the way the deer does.

MM: Wow! I never thought about being a deer while in school. But I could pretend. I could feel as if I was wearing a deer's ears instead of my own, and get the deer's ears to work for me. I will definitely add the "Pretending to Be an Animal" strategy to my strategy bank.

People Smart was in the playground with a group of friends.

PS: Magnificent, we are over here. You look puzzled or worried. Is something wrong?

MM: Well, I have been collecting listening strategies from the Smart Parts, and my strategy bank is pretty full. It is getting heavy.

MM: See, I have been having trouble with listening, so I started collecting strategies to improve. I was disappointing my teacher and my parents because I didn't have enough strategies in my bank. Can I share with you what I have learned so far? Maybe you have something to add.

★★★★★★★★★★★★★★★★★★★★

MM: Here is the "Listen to the Rhythm" strategy from Music Smart. I need to listen carefully to the music in the voice of the speaker, so I can tell what is really important.

MM: Here is the "Draw Pictures from Words" strategy from Picture Smart. I need to use my own paintbrush or camera or look through the photo album in my brain and visualize pictures that make the words I am hearing make sense to me.

MM: Body Smart gave me the "Moving Without Disturbing" strategy. I need to find ways to tap my foot in my shoe without moving my shoe, or move my muscles without anyone knowing.

MM: This one is the "Personalize It" strategy from Self Smart. I have to take what I am hearing and make it real to me by asking myself questions like how it makes me feel and whether I would do it that way. If I connect what I am hearing to things I care about, Self Smart says I will be able to get better at listening.

MM: I also got the "Make a New Word" strategy. Word Smart loves to make up words and can do it really quickly. This will be fun once I get better at it.

MM: Number Smart gave me the "Make a Formula" strategy, HATS. I need to *H*ear, *A*ssociate, *T*ranslate, and *S*tore. Then I will listen better.

MM: I got the "Pretending to be an Animal" strategy from Nature Smart. I can listen with deer's ears to what the teacher is saying.

★★★★★★★★★★★★★★★★★★★★

MM: What do you think?

PS: We think you have a great selection. Each Smart Part gave you something helpful. Now you just have to decide which strategies will work for you.

MM: Hmm. I think I could try all of them. Maybe I can use one strategy at a time until I figure out which ones work best. I think some might be more fun than others. Do you think any of the Smart Parts will feel bad if I don't use the strategy they gave me?

PS: No way. They will be happy if you find what works for you. Remember, everyone is different, and everyone should have their own strategy bank. Sometimes we can borrow strategies from others, but we often have to tweak them a little to make them our own. We usually use a combination of strategies when we are listening. Sometimes we use one, and sometimes we use another. But we thought of one that no one else gave you.

MM: What's that?

PS: We like to think about the speaker who is talking. We think about things like:

- ★ Why is this important to the speaker?
- ★ Where does the enthusiasm come from?
- ★ What do we like about the person?
- ★ How can we be more like this person?
- ★ How can we tell what this person thinks is really important?
- ★ What signals does the speaker give me about what he or she really cares about?

MM: You mean you try to analyze the speaker as a way to listen better?

PS: Sure. When we find a way to feel that the person cares about us, or is our friend, it makes it a lot easier to pay attention to what is being said.

MM: I can certainly add the "Make a Friend" strategy to my strategy bank. I never thought about it before, but I guess I do listen better to friends than I do to people I don't know or care about. Thanks, People Smart.

Magnificent Mind took all her strategies to school with her.

- ★ *She thought about them.*
- ★ *She practiced them.*
- ★ *She learned to use all of them.*

Magnificent found that she liked some strategies better than others. But she had so many strategies to choose from, she was able to find ones that really worked for her. By becoming mindful of the things she could do to listen, Magnificent found listening became easier and easier.

Magnificent Mind was proud of the way she used her mind to listen. And when you fill your strategy bank with strategies that work for you, you will feel proud of having such a magnificent mind, too.